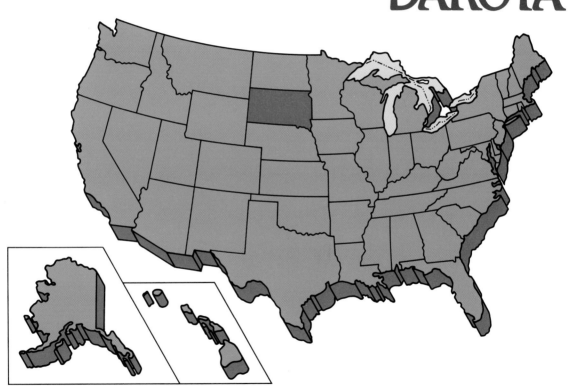

SOUTH DAKOTA

Hello U★S★A★

SOUTH DAKOTA

Karen Sirvaitis

Lerner Publications Company

LIBRARY OF CONGRESS
CATALOGING-IN-PUBLICATION DATA
Sirvaitis, Karen.
    South Dakota / by Karen Sirvaitis.
        p. cm. — (Hello USA)
    Includes index.
    ISBN 0-8225-2747-2 (lib. bdg.)
    1. South Dakota—Juvenile literature.
[1. South Dakota] I. Title II. Series.
F651.3.S57   1995
978.3—dc20   94-5451
                                          CIP
                                           AC

Manufactured in the United States of America

1 2 3 4 5 6 – I/JR – 00 99 98 97 96 95

Cover photograph courtesy of South Dakota Department of Tourism.

The glossary that begins on page 68 gives definitions of words shown in **bold type** in the text.

This book is printed on acid-free, recyclable paper.

CONTENTS

Did You Know . . . ?

❑ No one knows for sure whether South Dakota or North Dakota was the 39th state. On the same day in 1889, President Benjamin Harrison signed the admission papers for both states. Then he shuffled them so that nobody else would know which one was admitted first. The states are now ranked alphabetically, making South Dakota number 40.

❑ In 1972 heavy rains in Rapid City caused the worst flash flood in South Dakota's history. The flooding killed 237 people and damaged property worth $164 million.

Benjamin Harrison

❑ The longest tyrannosaur bones yet discovered were found near Faith, South Dakota, in 1990. The dinosaur was 40 feet (12 meters) long and probably weighed about 6 tons (5.4 metric tons) when it was alive.

6

❏ Sculptors used dynamite and drills to shape Mount Rushmore National Memorial near Rapid City, South Dakota. The mountainside carving, which features the faces of Presidents George Washington, Thomas Jefferson, Theodore Roosevelt, and Abraham Lincoln, stands 60 feet (18 m) tall. The noses alone are each about 20 feet (6 m) long.

❏ Tumbleweed did not exist in North America until the 1870s. Russian immigrants accidentally brought seeds of the spiny, sharp-leaved plant to South Dakota on their clothing. Settlers gave various names to tumbleweed, including Russian cactus, Russian thistle, and wind witch.

❏ Custer State Park in western South Dakota is home to about 1,400 bison, one of the largest publicly owned buffalo herds in the world.

A Trip Around the State

South Dakota, a rectangular state, is part of two different worlds. Considered a midwestern state, South Dakota is actually where the Midwest meets the West—where wheat fields give way to cattle ranches and where rolling hills lead to mountains.

The **prairies** and farms of neighboring Minnesota and Iowa advance into eastern South Dakota. The canyons and rangeland of Montana and Wyoming blend with western South Dakota. Endless miles of plains cover the central part of the state and stretch north into North Dakota and south into Nebraska.

Wind Cave National Park is located in southwestern South Dakota.

Flowering cactus

Purple coneflower

9

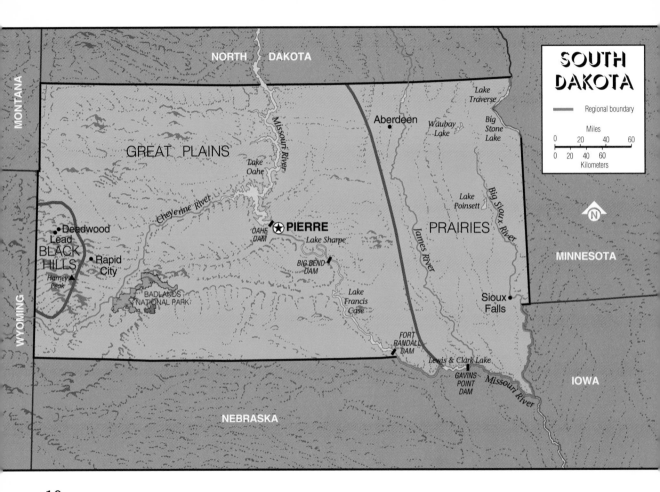

The regions within South Dakota are as different as the states surrounding it. From east to west, these regions are the Prairies, the Great Plains, and the Black Hills.

The Prairie region covers about one-fourth of South Dakota. More than 100 glistening lakes dot the northern part of the region, making it a popular vacation area.

Most of the lakes were formed by **glaciers.** These huge blocks of ice and snow moved across South Dakota thousands of years ago, gouging basins into the earth's surface. Gradually, rainwater and the melting ice of the glaciers filled the basins, creating lakes.

Gently rolling hills blanket much of the Prairies. Native grasses, some as high as 12 feet (4 m), once

Birds flock over Sand Lake in northeastern South Dakota.

coated the hills. Farmers plowed up this **grassland** in the late 1800s to plant crops in the fertile soil. Acres of wheat fields and corn stalks now rustle in the wind.

11

Native grasses blanket parts of the Great Plains.

The Great Plains region covers a large area of North America and crosses central and western South Dakota. Hills and valleys extend across South Dakota's plains. As in the Prairie region, the grassy plains have been plowed to make room for crops. In the western part of the state, the land becomes more rugged. **Buttes** (steep, flat-topped hills) tower over the surrounding plains, and canyons weave between the hillsides.

The Badlands cover about 100 miles (161 kilometers) of South Dakota's Great Plains. For thousands of years, wind and rain have worn away the soft, colorful rock of the Badlands, forming gullies, cliffs, and strangely shaped peaks.

13

South Dakota's most rugged landscape is in the Black Hills. From a distance, the region's thickly forested mountains appear to be black. Harney Peak, the state's highest point, reaches 7,242 feet (2,207 m) in the Black Hills.

The lowest point in South Dakota is Big Stone Lake, which lies along the Minnesota border in the Prairie region. Big Stone, Traverse, Waubay, and Poinsett are among the state's largest natural lakes. Dams along the Missouri River have created **reservoirs,** or artificial lakes, including Lakes Oahe, Francis Case, Sharpe, and Lewis and Clark.

The Missouri River is South Dakota's most important waterway. Freighters and barges cruise the

A path leads hikers up Harney Peak for a spectacular view of the Black Hills.

14

The Missouri River flows southward across the Great Plains, dividing South Dakota in half. South Dakotans refer to the two halves of their state as East River and West River.

river, carrying farm products and other goods to and from the state. Almost every river in South Dakota—including the Cheyenne, Big Sioux, and James—drains into the Missouri.

Some waterways in South Dakota may flood during the spring, dry up during the summer, or freeze during the winter—depending on the weather. The state's climate ranges from blistering hot to icy cold. Summer temperatures average 74° F (23° C), while average winter temperatures hover around 16° F (-9° C).

Eastern South Dakota and the Black Hills receive the most **precipitation** (rain and melted snow) in the state. Parts of South Dakota experience **droughts,** or long periods with little or no precipitation. During a drought, the farmland across the Prairies and the Great Plains turns dry and dusty, and, when the wind blows hard, a dust storm can cloud the air.

South Dakota receives an average of 18 inches (46 cm) of precipitation every year. This amount is enough for native grasses but does not support large plants such as shrubs and trees. Forests cover less than 4 percent of the state. The few trees in South Dakota grow mainly in the wetter Black Hills region and along riverbanks. The most common trees include pine, aspen, oak, and cottonwood.

Flowers such as poppies and black-eyed Susans color the plains in springtime. Bluebells, forget-me-nots, and flowering cactuses thrive in western South Dakota.

Prairie chicken

Pronghorn *(above)*   **Mountain goat** *(below)*

From prairie dogs to pronghorn, South Dakota is home to a variety of wild animals. Coyotes, as well as thousands of bison, inhabit the Great Plains. Elks and bighorn sheep climb ledges in the Black Hills. Beavers and raccoon live in eastern South Dakota, while bald eagles nest in the Badlands.

18

South Dakota's Story

The first people to settle in what is now South Dakota lived at least 10,000 years ago. Bones, tools, and weapons have been unearthed in the Black Hills region and along the Missouri River. These small pieces from the past reveal that the first South Dakotans used spears to hunt large mammals, including sloths and mammoths.

Thousands of years ago, millions of buffalo *(facing page)* **roamed the Missouri River valley.**

About 1,500 years ago, a group of Native Americans known as mound builders settled east of the Missouri River. These Indians are known for the large earthen burial mounds they built along the Big Sioux River and near Big Stone Lake.

Around A.D. 800, the Native Americans in what is now South Dakota stopped building mounds. No one is exactly sure what happened to the mound builders, but many researchers believe the Indians died from widespread disease.

Hundreds of years later, tribes that became known as the **Plains Indians** began to arrive in the northern Great Plains. The Arikara Indians canoed up the Missouri River to what is now South Dakota. They settled on the banks of the Missouri and Cheyenne rivers, where they built villages, hunted bison, and grew crops of corn, beans, and squash.

After the Arikara came the Cheyenne. Pushed westward by enemy nations, the Cheyenne also built villages, farmed, and hunted along the Missouri and Cheyenne rivers.

The Arikara and the Cheyenne often met on the banks of the Missouri River to trade furs, pottery, and beads. Every now and then, they also traded with strangely dressed men who spoke a very different language.

These men were French fur traders who exchanged pots, guns, and tools for beaver pelts, which sold for a high price in Europe. The Frenchmen claimed that France owned the trading grounds, along with much of North America's Great Plains. They called this huge

French fur traders sometimes offered Indians alcohol in exchange for furs.

Tepees were a familiar sight on the Great Plains after the 1700s. The Plains Indians brought the collapsible homes with them on long hunts.

area between the Missouri River and the Rocky Mountains the Louisiana Territory.

In 1743 two French Canadian brothers wrote about what is now South Dakota. François and Louis-Joseph La Vérendrye took notes about the Indians they met and about the plants and animals they saw while canoeing down the Missouri River.

Not long after the La Vérendrye expedition, the Sioux Indians were pushed westward into Arikara territory by their longtime rivals, the Ojibwa. The Sioux and the Arikara began fighting for control of the Missouri River valley. The Sioux defeated the Arikara and eventually spread throughout what is now South Dakota.

Sioux Family Tree

The Ojibwa Indians called their Sioux enemies *nadouessioux*—a kind of snake. French fur traders shortened the Ojibwa word to Sioux, and since then the name has been used to describe members of the Siouan-speaking nation.

Depending on what dialect they speak, the Sioux Indians call themselves Lakota, Dakota, or Nakota—Siouan words for ally, or friend. Each of these dialects is associated with a political group. The Lakota are the Teton, the Nakota are the Yankton, and the Dakota are the Santee.

The three branches of Sioux are divided further into smaller groups called bands. Sioux Indians are often identified with the name of their branch or band—an Oglala Sioux (from the Oglala band of the Teton), a Teton Sioux, or a Lakota, for example.

In the 1700s and 1800s, the Lakota hunted buffalo in the western Dakotas and in Nebraska. The Dakota lived in Minnesota, while the Nakota farmed in the eastern Dakotas, Minnesota, and Iowa.

Meanwhile, U.S. president Thomas Jefferson bought the Louisiana Territory from France. The Louisiana Purchase, which took place in 1803, doubled the size of the United States.

Jefferson sent an expedition, led by Meriwether Lewis and William Clark, to explore the new possession. In 1804 Lewis and Clark reached what is now South Dakota, where they camped along the Big Sioux and the Missouri rivers. The men met Indians from various tribes and saw plants and animals they had never heard of before. When the explorers returned home in 1806, they reported finding beavers and other fur-bearing animals in what is now South Dakota.

Encouraged by the news, fur traders soon headed for the Great Plains. Although Lewis and Clark had generally gotten along well with tribes they came in contact with, the relationship between the fur traders and the Indians was sometimes difficult. In 1823 the Arikara attacked and killed 13 U.S. fur traders.

To help protect fur traders, the U.S. Army sent troops, who were aided by Sioux Indians, to drive the Arikara northward. These soldiers were the first of many to come.

Fort Pierre, originally called Fort Tecumseh, was founded in 1823 as a trading post. Fur traders and Sioux Indians gathered at this center to exchange blankets, clothing, household goods, furs, and hides.

By 1850 most of the beavers had been killed, ending the fur-trading boom in what is now South Dakota. But another kind of settler was attracted to the area—the farmer.

In the mid-1800s, people from the eastern United States ventured west seeking good farmland. Some of these pioneers built farms on the fertile soils in what is now southeastern South Dakota—the homeland of a branch of Sioux Indians called the Yankton.

To avoid any chance of warfare against the newcomers, the Yankton Sioux ceded the region to the U.S. government in 1858. In exchange, the Indians received money, supplies, and 400,000 acres (162,000 hectares) of **reservation** land. The government promised that the settlers would not disturb the Indians on the reservation.

Before long, farmers and businesspeople were pouring into the newly opened area. They built the towns of Yankton, Vermillion, and Bon Homme. In 1861 the U.S. government established the Dakota Territory, which included the present states of North and South Dakota and parts of Wyoming and Montana. The territory was named after the Dakota (or Sioux) Indians.

The surge of settlers to the Dakota Territory did not last long. In fact, in the following few years about half the pioneers left their stores, towns, and fields behind.

The pioneers were frightened by what became known as the Minnesota Uprising (1862–1866). The

In all, nearly 600 people died in the Minnesota Uprising.

Santee Sioux in Minnesota, angry that so many newcomers were farming Indian land, began raiding white settlements. When the attacks spread into the Dakota Territory, many of the pioneers fled, returning only after U.S. troops ended the conflict.

The discovery of gold in Montana stirred up more conflict. Thousands of prospectors crossed the Dakota Territory to get to the goldfields. One explorer, John Bozeman, found a shortcut through Sioux homelands. When the U.S. government built forts to protect travelers along the Bozeman Trail, the Sioux attacked the forts.

The Indians were successful. In 1868 the U.S. government signed a **treaty,** or agreement, stating that the trail would not be used. In addition, all pioneers west of the Missouri River had to leave. The entire region became the Great Sioux Reservation—property of the Sioux nation.

Red Cloud, a warrior and chief of the Oglala Sioux, led attacks against forts along the Bozeman Trail. The effort to close the trail is sometimes called Red Cloud's War.

After the treaty, most of the Indians in the Dakota Territory lived on the reservation. Battles and attacks ended, and farmers were again attracted to the rich soils east of the Missouri River.

Some of the farmers were **immigrants** from Denmark, Norway, Sweden, and Germany who came to the Dakota Territory to benefit from the Homestead Act. Through this act, the U.S. government gave 160 acres (65 hectares) of land to each pioneer family willing to plow the prairie. These settlers became known as homesteaders.

In the early 1870s, the farmers of Dakota Territory battled something they could not settle by treaty—grasshopper raids. Millions of grasshoppers invaded the territory's cropland every July for four years. As small as they were, the insects destroyed entire crops and drove many farmers out of the territory for good. Some settlers braved the hard years, waiting for better times.

Little House from the Prairie

South Dakotans living in areas of treeless grassland lacked a lumber supply. But the roots of the prairie grasses were so solid that these homesteaders, also known as sodbusters, used blocks of sod (or grass) as a building material for their homes.

Called soddies, the houses were cheap to construct. The average soddie consisted of one acre of sod, a couple of windows, and a door. The total cost—about $5 or $10. The homes did not burn down during prairie fires, and they kept out most of the snow, rain, and wind-blown dust. But they were also uncomfortable. Dirt fell from the ceilings, and animals, such as gophers and snakes, burrowed through the floors.

Many sodbusters dreamed of the day they would earn a profit from their crops and could afford to buy lumber shipped in from woodlands. But others dwelled in their practical soddies long after wood-frame homes became common on the prairie.

Hoppers by the Hordes

Grasshoppers, the most numerous insect on the prairie, have always been a bother to South Dakotans. The grasshopper raids of the 1870s, however, were caused by a type of hopper that no longer exists in the United States—the migratory locust. For migratory locusts to have become a problem to farmers and ranchers, certain environmental conditions had to be ripe.

A grasshopper's chance of survival, for instance, improves dramatically during a drought. A dry autumn extends the egg-laying season, allowing a female hopper to lay more eggs than usual. Disease, which spreads quickly in humid weather, is not a major killer of locusts during a drought. And if birds leave an area that is hit by drought to find food and water elsewhere, locusts have fewer enemies.

During the drought of the 1870s, a swarm of migratory locusts rose near the Rocky Mountains. Aided by the wind, they headed east toward the Great Plains. The warm weather encouraged them to become active. They traveled together and when one swarm met another, dense hordes developed. Some hordes were miles long, miles wide, and miles deep.

When the hoppers stopped to eat, they consumed whatever was in their path, including crops, tree bark, and clothes. Farmers and ranchers did their best to stop the insects with fire, but the numbers—which had reached the billions—were too great.

As the locusts approached the more humid climate in the east, their chances of survival decreased. Predators and disease helped reduce the size of the horde, which eventually died out naturally.

In 1874 Custer's expedition made its camp on French Creek in the Black Hills, just south of what is now the city of Custer.

In 1874 the U.S. Army sent Lieutenant Colonel George Armstrong Custer and 1,200 soldiers, scientists, and miners to the Black Hills to study the area's geography and natural resources. Custer was also required to build a fort to prevent settlers from entering the Great Sioux Reservation.

Word got out that Custer's expedition had found gold, and hundreds of gold seekers poured into the Black Hills. The U.S. government volunteered to pay the Sioux for the right to mine the region. But the Black Hills were sacred to the Indians, and they refused the offer. Custer and his troops withdrew, leaving the Indians and the miners to fend for themselves.

Shortly after being founded in 1876, Deadwood *(above)* **was home to more than 20,000 miners** *(inset)* **and merchants.**

The miners built several towns near the major gold strikes in the Black Hills. In 1876 these illegal settlements on Sioux land helped spark the War for the Black Hills.

U.S. troops started the fighting by pursuing a group of Sioux who would not live on the reservation. These Indians were refusing to sacrifice their traditional ways for reservation life.

The major battles of the war took place in what are now Montana and Wyoming, but the Indians occasionally attacked miners in the Black Hills. At the war's end, the Sioux were forced to sign a new treaty, giving up the Black Hills region of their reservation.

Sitting Bull, a Sioux medicine man born in South Dakota, was among the Indians who refused to live on a reservation. Sitting Bull spiritually guided Crazy Horse, who defeated Custer in the Battle of the Little Bighorn (which took place in what is now Montana)—the most famous battle during the War for the Black Hills. Crazy Horse, who never allowed his photograph to be taken, is not pictured.

In the 1880s, the Black Hills drew more miners and also ranchers, who found plenty of grazing land for their cattle and sheep. The ranchers supplied meat to local towns and to the Indians. Once railroads crossed the Dakota Territory, the ranchers also shipped their livestock to the East Coast to be slaughtered and sold.

By 1889 the Dakota Territory had enough white people to become a state. The U.S. government split the territory in two, admitting North Dakota and South Dakota to the Union as separate states.

After miners arrived in the Black Hills, sheep and cattle ranchers came to supply meat.

LET THE
Eagle Scream!
PIERRE!
— IS THE —
PLACE!

The beginning of South Dakota's statehood marked the end of the Great Sioux Reservation. In 1889 the United States asked the Sioux to give up most of their land. To avoid war, the Indians agreed to settle on smaller reservations.

But bloodshed came in 1890 during the Massacre at Wounded Knee, the last major conflict between U.S. troops and Plains Indians. Knowing that their traditional way of life was coming to an end, many Sioux Indians had begun to practice a new religion called the Ghost Dance. Followers of the Ghost Dance believed that health and happiness would come to Indians only if people lived in peace. U.S. military officials, suspicious of the large religious gatherings, ordered the Sioux Indians to stop practicing the Ghost Dance.

In 1889 Pierre was one of many towns competing to become the capital of South Dakota.

Sitting Bull introduced the Sioux to the Ghost Dance in 1890. This religion was expressed through rhythmic movement.

The Sioux who refused to quit fled to the Badlands, where they were captured by U.S. troops and taken to Wounded Knee Creek. When a gun accidentally went off among the prisoners, the soldiers reacted, filling the air with a thunderous blare of cannon fire and gunfire. Hundreds of Indians died, along with 30 U.S. soldiers.

South Dakota's first years of statehood also were troubled by a period of drought known as the Great Dakota Bust. Unable to make a living from farming the parched land, many settlers left the state. Newcomers arrived after the drought ended in 1897 and as more Indian lands were opened to settlement. To encourage even more pioneers to come to South Dakota, the U.S. government greatly increased the number of acres a homesteader could claim.

South Dakota's farmers made a good profit supplying meat, vegetables, and grains to troops fighting overseas during World War I (1914–1918). Crops sold for high prices during the war, so farmers plowed up more of their land to plant wheat and corn.

Many farmers bought new equipment during the prosperous farming years of the 1910s.

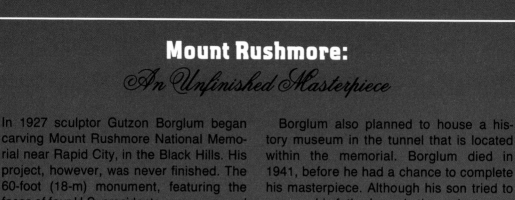

Mount Rushmore:
An Unfinished Masterpiece

In 1927 sculptor Gutzon Borglum began carving Mount Rushmore National Memorial near Rapid City, in the Black Hills. His project, however, was never finished. The 60-foot (18-m) monument, featuring the faces of four U.S. presidents, was supposed to include their waists.

Borglum also planned to house a history museum in the tunnel that is located within the memorial. Borglum died in 1941, before he had a chance to complete his masterpiece. Although his son tried to carry on his father's work, the project came to a halt when the U.S. government ran out of funds for the memorial during World War II.

During the drought of the 1930s, heavy winds stripped fields of topsoil, carrying it for miles and burying homes and automobiles.

During the 1930s, farmers in South Dakota again saw hard times. Almost 10 straight years of drought and dust storms, along with several grasshopper raids, ravaged crops. On top of that, South Dakotans were suffering through the Great Depression, a major slump in the nation's economy. During the depression, banks failed, businesses closed, and many workers lost their jobs.

The Great Depression came to an end during World War II (1939–1945), when South Dakota's farmers were again called on to supply food to troops overseas. The U.S. government also built the Ellsworth Air Force Base (near Rapid City) and the Sioux Falls Air Force Training Base. These bases created jobs for South Dakotans.

The Spirit of Crazy Horse

Korczak Ziolkowski (1909–1982) stands behind his model of the Crazy Horse Memorial.

Only 17 miles (27 km) south of Mount Rushmore, the budding image of Sioux leader Crazy Horse astride his horse marks Thunderhead Mountain in the Black Hills. At the request of Sioux chief Henry Standing Bear, the Crazy Horse Memorial was started in 1948 by sculptor Korczak Ziolkowski, who dedicated much of his life to the project.

Once it is completed sometime after the year 2000, the memorial will be the largest sculpture in the world, reaching 563 feet (172 m) in height and 641 feet (195 m) in width. In addition to the carving, a medical university and a permanent building for the Indian Museum of North America are planned for the site.

After the war, the U.S. government hired workers to build four dams on the Missouri River in South Dakota. Called the Pick-Sloan Missouri Basin Program, the dams controlled flooding, supplied water to cities and farms, and powered engines that produced electricity. The four reservoirs created by the dams became known as the Great Lakes of South Dakota.

In 1973 a group of Indians took over the village of Wounded Knee on the Pine Ridge Indian Reservation for 71 days. The Native Americans were protesting the leadership of Richard Wilson, president of the Oglala Sioux. They also hoped to gain fairer treatment of Indians across the country. Two Indians were killed, dozens of people were injured, and hundreds were arrested before the group surrendered to U.S. forces.

The fight for land, leadership, and freedom in South Dakota has moved from the battlefield to the courthouse. In 1980 the U.S. Supreme Court ordered the U.S. government to pay the Sioux more than $120 million for land seized in the Black Hills region in 1876. The Indians have refused the money. Instead, they want one million acres (405,000 hectares) of the Black Hills returned to them.

In 1989 South Dakota celebrated 100 years of statehood, causing many South Dakotans to think about their history. Some people may have imagined their ancestors leaving their village on horseback to hunt a stampeding herd of bison. Others told family stories of droughts and grasshopper raids or dreamt about mining gold. South Dakota is a young state, but it has a long, rich past.

| 8,000 B.C. | A.D. 500 | 1743 | 1803 |

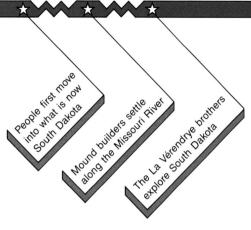

People first move into what is now South Dakota

Mound builders settle along the Missouri River

The La Vérendrye brothers explore South Dakota

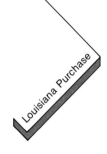

Louisiana Purchase

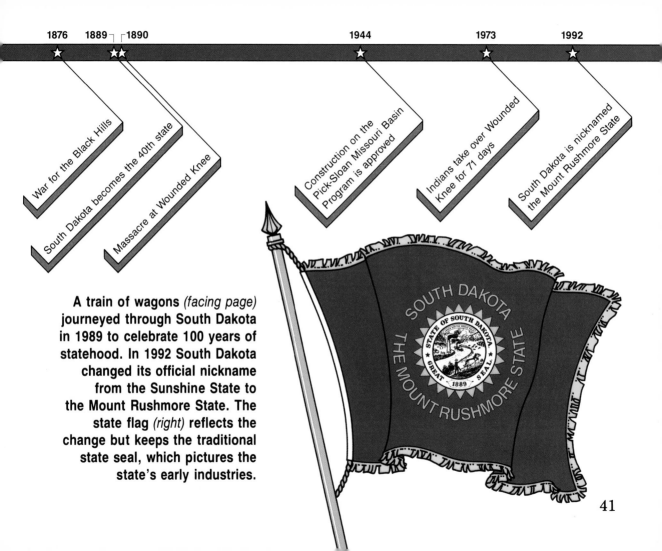

1876 — War for the Black Hills

1889 — South Dakota becomes the 40th state

1890 — Massacre at Wounded Knee

1944 — Construction on the Pick-Sloan Missouri Basin Program is approved

1973 — Indians take over Wounded Knee for 71 days

1992 — South Dakota is nicknamed the Mount Rushmore State

A train of wagons *(facing page)* **journeyed through South Dakota in 1989 to celebrate 100 years of statehood. In 1992 South Dakota changed its official nickname from the Sunshine State to the Mount Rushmore State. The state flag** *(right)* **reflects the change but keeps the traditional state seal, which pictures the state's early industries.**

41

Living and Working in South Dakota

Most South Dakotans grow up on farms, on ranches, or in small towns. Some of South Dakota's 696,000 residents still work the land their families homesteaded in the late 1800s and early 1900s.

About 1 out of 12 workers in South Dakota has a job in agriculture—a large number compared to most other states. Livestock brings in the most money for South Dakota's farmers and ranchers.

Ranchers drive a herd of cattle along a mountain road in the Black Hills.

Dairy cattle, chickens, turkeys, and geese are found throughout the Prairie region, while sheep and beef cattle graze the pastures of the Great Plains. Bison, nearly extinct 100 years ago, are now being raised on ranches. The ranchers hope to someday sell their bison meat to restaurants and grocery stores around the world.

South Dakota's leading crops are corn, wheat, and sunflowers. Rainfall is so undependable in South Dakota that farmers channel water from the ground and from reservoirs to their fields. This process, called **irrigation,** has saved many crops during the state's frequent droughts.

Some people choose bison meat instead of beef, which is higher in fat and cholesterol.

Many farms *(left)* **in South Dakota grow sunflowers** *(above).* **The seeds of sunflowers are used to make vegetable oil, snack food, and bird seed.**

Crops and livestock are taken to the state's food-processing companies, where workers package meat and dairy products and grind grain into flour or livestock feed. Some South Dakotans build farm machinery. Other kinds of goods made in the state include aircraft parts, lumber products, and gold jewelry. About 1 in every 10 working South Dakotans has a job in manufacturing.

45

Mines throughout the state employ only 1 percent of South Dakota's workforce. The Homestake Gold Mine in the Black Hills produces the most gold in the state. Western South Dakota also yields large amounts of oil.

The people who sell South Dakota's minerals have what are called service jobs. People with service jobs also include bankers, park rangers, doctors, and soldiers. Service businesses employ three out of four of the state's workers.

The Homestake Gold Mine in Lead has been producing gold for more than 100 years.

Children from the Pine Ridge Indian Reservation enjoy an amusement park ride.

e Americans in South Da- mber just over 50,000— percent of the state's total ion. Nearly half of the Na- ericans in South Dakota he state's nine Indian res- s. These include two of the eservations in the United -Pine Ridge and Cheyenne

In the Black Hills, not too far from the Pine Ridge Indian Reservation, sculptors are building a memorial to Crazy Horse, one of the greatest leaders in Sioux history. When it is finished, the Crazy Horse Memorial will stand 563 feet (172 m) high and 641 feet (195 m) long. It will be the largest statue in the world.

Some of South Dakota's government workers have offices in the state capitol building in Pierre.

South Dakota's service jobs are found mostly in the state's largest cities, which include Sioux Falls, Rapid City, and Aberdeen. Many government service workers, including the governor, live in the state capital of Pierre.

Most Sout... cestors from Denmark, Ca Germany, a Americans, Americans ea 1 percent of t

Nati kota n about 7 popula tive A live on ervatio largest States- River.

48

In 1991 South Dakota celebrated the 50th anniversary of another Black Hills attraction, the Mount Rushmore National Memorial. One year later, South Dakota's nickname was changed from the Sunshine State to the Mount Rushmore State.

Another attraction in the Black Hills region is Flintstones Bedrock City, a park where visitors can catch a glimpse of the Stone Age and eat Bronto Burgers and Dino Dogs. The Wild West is remembered in Deadwood and Lead, towns where the nation's last great gold rush took place in 1876.

At the Cultural Heritage Center in Pierre, visitors see how an early mining operation worked.

Different designs made of corn, including one of Mount Rushmore National Memorial, line the walls of the Corn Palace.

In eastern South Dakota, Mitchell is home to the Corn Palace. Inside and outside, the walls of the palace are decorated with thousands of bushels of native corn and grasses. Every September the Corn Palace Festival celebrates harvesttime with parades and food.

Northeast of Mitchell lies De Smet, the town made famous by author Laura Ingalls Wilder. In a series of popular children's books, Wilder described growing up on the prairie in the late 1800s. Her original South Dakota home still stands, surrounded by cottonwood trees that were planted by the Ingalls family.

Festivals featuring traditional Native American arts and crafts include the Indian art show in Pine Ridge and the Sioux Falls Northern Plains Tribal Arts Show. The Oscar Howe Art Center in Mitchell displays the paintings of Oscar Howe, a famous Sioux artist.

Towns throughout South Dakota are proud of their historic sites and museums. The Prairie

Visitors can view the parlor of the Ingalls home in De Smet.

Homestead Historic Site near Badlands National Park displays original homestead buildings. At the Black Hills Mining Museum in Lead, visitors can see how mining has changed over the years and can even pan for gold.

Climbers scale the steep slopes of Beaver Creek Gorge in Wind Cave National Park.

Just outside Rapid City, the South Dakota Air & Space Museum at Ellsworth Air Force Base exhibits old bomber and fighter planes. A separate building houses historic military uniforms. The South Dakota Art Museum in Brookings features the work of some of the state's most famous artists.

For those who prefer the open air, the Black Hills region offers ski slopes, hiking trails, and lakes and streams for fishing. The Great Lakes of South Dakota along the Missouri River are popular among boaters, fishers, and swimmers.

Along the eastern edge of the Black Hills lie Custer State Park and Wind Cave National Park, where large herds of bison graze freely. In nearby Badlands National Park, hikers can examine the remains of ancient animals that once roamed the region. The bones of three-toed horses, prehistoric camels, and saber-toothed tigers are preserved in the area's colorful cliffs.

The remains of prehistoric animals can be found in Hot Springs, South Dakota. The animals, trapped in a limestone pit, died of starvation more than 10,000 years ago.

Protecting the Environment

Corn is a leading crop grown on South Dakota's grasslands.

Farmers in the grasslands of South Dakota and other states have provided the nation with most of its food for more than 100 years. Some of the farming methods used over the years have robbed the region's once rich soil of nutrients and have exposed millions of tons of topsoil to blowing winds. Some experts predict that the grasslands will soon be ruined unless farmers continue to improve their methods and unless researchers develop stronger varieties of crops.

Wheat grown on the Great Plains helps feed the world.

Farmers have known for a long time that different crops absorb different nutrients from the soil. Farmers also know that if they change the type of crop they plant every year—a practice called **crop rotation**—the soil is enriched. But sometimes the U.S. government encourages farmers to sow a certain crop, such as wheat, year after year by paying high prices for it. Many farmers cannot earn enough money to continue farming unless they plant the high-paying crop. This practice discourages crop rotation and, over time, the quality of the soil is reduced.

56

More than 7,000 types of grasses exist in the world. Some—such as wheat, corn, barley, and rye—are grown as crops, and others are used on lawns. A native grass called little bluestem *(inset)* once thrived on South Dakota's Great Plains.

Before large numbers of farmers came to South Dakota, Native Americans grew a limited number of crops that hardly even affected the grasslands. Thousands of different types of native grasses covered the area. Tallgrasses, reaching at least 5 feet (1.5 m) high, spanned the eastern strip of South Dakota's Prairie region, where rainfall was the most plentiful. A variety of short, medium, and tall plants called mixed-grasses grew over the Great Plains.

Native grasses are excellent for the soil. When native grasses die they decay, adding valuable nutrients to the soil. The great variety of native plants once found on the grasslands enriched the soil with many different kinds of nutrients.

57

Bison are among the largest animals on South Dakota's prairie. Each year, one bison needs up to 100 acres (40 hectares) of grasses to survive.

These durable, fast-growing native plants also provide food and homes to all kinds of wildlife—including pronghorn, prairie dogs, and bison. The large numbers of animals that once roamed the plains consumed huge amounts of grass, which encouraged more grass to grow by exposing new shoots to sunshine.

The prairie wildlife also gave new sprouts a chance to bud by turning up soil with their hooves and claws. This process loosened the soil, allowing roots to grow and helping nutrients and water soak into the soil.

Native grasses and wildlife disappeared acre by acre as farmers plowed the prairie. They broke up the sod and planted non-native grasses, such as wheat and corn. Unlike the native grasses, these cultivated crops could not always survive South Dakota's harsh weather. During droughts, crops either died or failed to sprout. The rich topsoil—once held down firmly by the solid roots of native grasses—was exposed and sometimes blown away by the wind.

After harvesting their crops, farmers plowed up the stubble, leaving the land bare. With no grasses left to decay and add nutrients, the quality of the soil became poor. To ensure a good harvest the following year, farmers fertilized their crops with costly chemical nutrients. Fertilizers can pollute soil and water and can increase the cost of farming.

Drought kills crops and leaves soil unprotected from the sun and wind.

To save their soil, some South Dakotans are choosing methods that are better for the land. Farmers help hold soil in place by leaving crop stubble on the ground and by plowing their fields in patterns that help block the wind. By rotat-

ing crops, farmers are deciding to lose money in the short run to preserve their land in the long run.

Many people agree that a change in how the prices for crops are determined—not just a change in farming methods—is also necessary. Many farmers want to be able to afford to plant crops that help preserve soil, even though those crops may not bring in the most money.

Some experts believe that replanting native grasses is the best way to save the soil of the grasslands for future generations. Re-

A researcher examines the grasses that now protect the soil of this former cropland. Poor farming methods and harsh weather had made the land unsuitable for farming.

searchers could then study native grasses to develop new varieties of crops that would feed millions of people and at the same time conserve and enrich the soil. By developing new grasses, South Dakotans may be able to save both the grasslands and their farmland.

South Dakota's Famous People

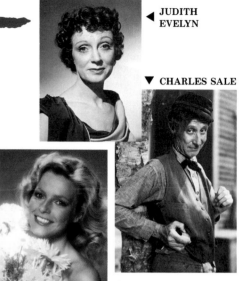

◄ JUDITH EVELYN

▼ CHARLES SALE

ACTORS

Judith Evelyn (1913–1967) was best known for her portrayals of high-strung women. Among her stage credits are *Angel Street*, *A Streetcar Named Desire*, and *Pygmalion*. Born in Seneca, South Dakota, Evelyn also appeared in several films, including *The Brothers Karamazov* and *Rear Window*.

Cheryl Ladd (born 1951), from Huron, South Dakota, became famous when she costarred as a detective on the popular 1970s television series "Charlie's Angels." Ladd's film credits include *Grace Kelly* and *Now and Forever*.

Charles ("Chic") Sale (1885–1936), born in Huron, South Dakota, was an actor whose specialty was playing odd characters. His most famous film appearances include *Star Witness*, *Treasure Island*, and *It's a Great Life*.

◄ CHERYL LADD

▼ TOM BROKAW

▲ MARY HART

ANCHORS

Tom Brokaw (born 1940) is recognized by millions of Americans as the anchor on "NBC Nightly News." Before taking the position in 1982, Brokaw hosted NBC's early morning news program, the "Today" show. He was raised in Webster, South Dakota.

Mary Hart (born 1950) is cohost of the weeknight television program "Entertainment Tonight," which features news about the music and film industries. Hart, who has cohosted since 1982, is from Sioux Falls, South Dakota.

ARTISTS

Oscar Howe (1915–1983), an internationally known Yankton Sioux artist, painted in a unique style that reflected the traditional values and beliefs of the Sioux. Howe, born on the Crow Creek Reservation in South Dakota, taught creative art at the University of South Dakota.

Roy Justus (1901–1984) was an internationally recognized political cartoonist from Avon, South Dakota. During his 50-year career, Justus drew cartoons that delivered messages about topics ranging from nuclear weapons to population growth.

Jess Thomas (born 1927) is an opera singer from Hot Springs, South Dakota. The tenor made his first appearance with the New York Metropolitan Opera in 1962. Since then Thomas has sung with major opera companies around the world.

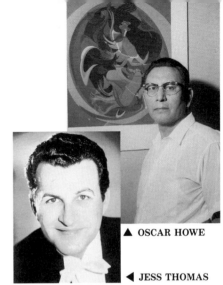

▲ OSCAR HOWE

◄ JESS THOMAS

RUSSELL ▶
MEANS

NATIVE AMERICAN LEADERS

Crazy Horse (1844?–1877), born on Rapid Creek in the Black Hills of South Dakota, fought to recapture Sioux land taken by the U.S. government. Crazy Horse's Sioux name (Tashunca-uitco) is more accurately translated as Unbroken Horse.

Russell Means (born 1939) was a leader of the American Indian Movement (AIM), an organization dedicated to fighting for the rights of Native Americans, from 1969 to 1988. Born on the Pine Ridge Indian Reservation in South Dakota, Means participated in the 71-day seige of Wounded Knee in 1973. He also starred in the film *The Last of the Mohicans*.

63

Hubert Humphrey (1911–1978) served as vice president of the United States in the 1960s under Lyndon B. Johnson. Born in Wallace, South Dakota, Humphrey later moved to Minnesota, the state he represented as a U.S. senator both before and after his term as vice president.

George McGovern (born 1922), from Avon, South Dakota, served his state for more than 20 years as a U.S. representative and as a U.S. senator. In 1972 McGovern ran for U.S. president and lost the election to Richard Nixon.

◀ HUBERT HUMPHREY

GEORGE McGOVERN ▶

◀ ALTON OCHSNER

Alton Ochsner (1896–1981), was a native of Kimball, South Dakota. In the 1940s, he became one of the first physicians to link smoking with lung cancer. The world-famous heart surgeon also cofounded a clinic, which later became part of the Ochsner Medical Institutions in New Orleans, Louisiana.

Merle Tuve (1901–1982) received many awards for his scientific research, which helped lead to the development of radar and to the understanding of nuclear energy. Tuve was born in Canton, South Dakota.

SPARKY ▶
ANDERSON

George Lee ("Sparky") Anderson (born 1934), former manager of the Cincinnati Reds baseball team, has managed the Detroit Tigers since 1979. Anderson, born in Bridgewater,

South Dakota, is the first manager in major league baseball to win more than 800 games with two different teams. He is also the first manager ever to win a World Series in both the American and National leagues.

Norm Van Brocklin (1926–1983) was a professional football player from Eagle Butte, South Dakota. He played quarterback for the Los Angeles Rams and the Philadelphia Eagles before coaching the Minnesota Vikings and the Atlanta Falcons. Van Brocklin was elected into the Football Hall of Fame in 1971.

VERA CLEAVER ▶

▼ VINE DELORIA, JR.

ROSE WILDER ▶ LANE

WRITERS

Vera Cleaver (born 1919), from Virgil, South Dakota, is an award-winning author of children's books, many of which she writes with her husband, Bill. Her titles include *Ellen Grae, Moon Lake Angel,* and *Where the Lilies Bloom.*

Vine Deloria, Jr. (born 1933), a Sioux educator, lawyer, and author, is dedicated to the struggle for Native American rights. Among his books are *Custer Died for Your Sins: An Indian Manifesto, God is Red,* and *Behind the Trail of Broken Treaties.* He is originally from Martin, South Dakota.

Rose Wilder Lane (1887–1968) was a writer born to pioneers in De Smet, South Dakota. Her most famous novel, *Let the Hurricane Roar,* is for children. Lane cowrote *On the Way Home* with her mother, Laura Ingalls Wilder, who is best known as the author of *Little House on the Prairie* and other popular children's books.

65

Facts-at-a-Glance

Nickname: Mount Rushmore State
Song: "Hail, South Dakota"
Motto: Under God the People Rule
Flower: American pasqueflower
Tree: Black Hills spruce
Bird: ring-necked pheasant

Population: 696,004*
Rank in population, nationwide: 45th
Area: 77,121 square miles
Rank in area, nationwide: 17th
Date and ranking of statehood:
   November 2, 1889, the 40th state
Capital: Pierre (12,906*)
Major cities (and populations*):
   Sioux Falls (100,814), Rapid City (54,523),
   Aberdeen (24,927), Watertown (17,592)
U.S. senators: 2
U.S. representatives: 1
Electoral votes: 3

Places to visit: Mount Rushmore National Memorial near Rapid City, Crazy Horse Memorial in the Black Hills, Corn Palace in Mitchell, Wall Drug Store in Wall, Jewel Cave National Monument near Custer

Annual events: Schmeckfest in Freeman (March–April), Laura Ingalls Wilder Pageant in De Smet (June–July), Folk Art Festival in Brookings (July), Days of '76 in Deadwood (Aug.), South Dakota and Open Fiddlers' Jamboree in Yankton (Sept.)

*1990 census

66

Natural resources: fertile soil, gold, oil, natural gas, stone, sand and gravel, silver, clay

Agricultural products: cattle, wheat, hogs, corn, soybeans, sunflower seeds, hay, oats, sheep

Manufactured goods: meat and dairy products, flour, livestock feed, farm and construction equipment, medical instruments, cooking appliances, newspapers

ENDANGERED SPECIES
Mammals—black-footed ferret
Birds—bald eagle, Eskimo curlew, interior least tern, whooping crane
Fish—banded killifish, central mudminnow, pallid sturgeon, pearl dace

WHERE SOUTH DAKOTANS WORK
Services—54 percent
    (services includes jobs in trade; community, social, & personal services; finance, insurance, & real estate; transportation, communication, & utilities)
Government—20 percent
Agriculture—12 percent
Manufacturing—10 percent
Construction—3 percent
Mining—1 percent

MIN
1%
CONST
3%
MFG
10%
AGR
12%
SERVICES
54%
GOVT
20%

Glossary

butte An isolated hill or mountain with steep sides.

crop rotation Alternating the crops grown in a field from one year to the next to replace the minerals taken from the soil by one type of crop.

drought A long period of extreme dryness due to lack of rain or snow.

glacier A large body of ice and snow that moves slowly over land.

grassland A region in which grasses are the natural form of plant life. Cultivated grasses, such as corn and wheat, may be grown in the region. In the United States, grasslands are also called prairies and meadows.

immigrant A person who moves to a foreign country and settles there.

irrigation A method of watering land by directing water through canals, ditches, pipes, or sprinklers.

Plains Indians Indian nations that lived on the Great Plains (a region covering much of central North America) and that shared similar traditions.

prairie A large area of level or gently rolling grassy land with few trees.

precipitation Rain, snow, and other forms of moisture that fall to earth.

reservation Public land set aside by the government to be used by Native Americans.

reservoir A place where water is collected and stored for later use.

treaty An agreement between two or more groups, usually having to do with peace or trade.

Index

Acknowledgments:

Maryland Cartographics, Inc., pp. 2, 10; Jerry Hennen, pp. 2–3, 9 (bottom), 40, 50, 54, 56–57; Library of Congress, pp. 6, 18, 20; Jack Lindstrom, p. 7; Kent & Donna Dannen, pp. 8–9, 14, 17 (top right), 51, 52, 53; Mark Kayser / South Dakota Dept. of Tourism, pp. 9 (top), 17 (top left), 58, 71; Glacial Lakes and Prairies of Northeastern South Dakota, p. 11; USDA Forest Service, p. 12; Lia E. Munson / Root Resources, p. 13; South Dakota Dept. of Tourism, pp. 15, 45 (left), 49; Chad Coppess / South Dakota Dept. of Tourism, pp. 16, 17 (bottom), 45 (right), 47, 48, 69; South Dakota Historical Society—State Archives, pp. 23, 27, 29, 30 (both), 32, 33; Minnesota Historical Society, p. 25; Smithsonian Institution National Anthropological Archives, Bureau of American Ethnology Collection, pp. 26, 31; Center for Western Studies, p. 34; Siouxland Heritage Museums, p. 35; Jerome Rogers, p. 36; National Archives, Am Im 133; © Korczak's Heritage, Inc., p. 38; Buddy Mays / Travel Stock, pp. 42–43, 55, 59; Lynn M. Stone, p. 44; Homestake Mining Co., p. 46; David Dvorak, Jr., p. 57 (inset); Karelle Scharff, p. 60; South Dakota Department of Agriculture, p. 61; Museum of Modern Art / Film Stills Archive, p. 62 (top, center right); Hollywood Book & Poster Co., p. 62 (center left, bottom left, bottom right); State University, Vermillion, S.D., p. 63 (top right); Metropolitan Opera Archives, p. 63 (top left); Johnny Sundby, p. 63 (bottom); Marty Nordstrom, Minnesota Historical Society, p. 64 (top left); George McGovern, p. 64 (top right); Ochsner Medical Institutions, New Orleans, p. 64 (center); Detroit Tigers, p. 64 (bottom); LA Rams, p. 65 (top); Harper Collins, p. 65 (center right); Vine Deloria, Jr., p. 65 (center left); Laura Ingalls Wilder Home & Museum, p. 65 (bottom); Jean Matheny, p. 66.